PIANO - VOCAL - GUITAR

BEST OF
JANET JACKSON

Cover photo by Paul Bergin/Redferns

ISBN 978-1-4234-2687-5

HAL•LEONARD®
CORPORATION
7777 W. BLUEMOUND RD. P.O. BOX 13819 MILWAUKEE, WI 53213

Visit Hal Leonard Online at
www.halleonard.com

AGAIN
Written for the Motion Picture POETIC JUSTICE

Words and Music by JANET JACKSON,
JAMES HARRIS III and TERRY LEWIS

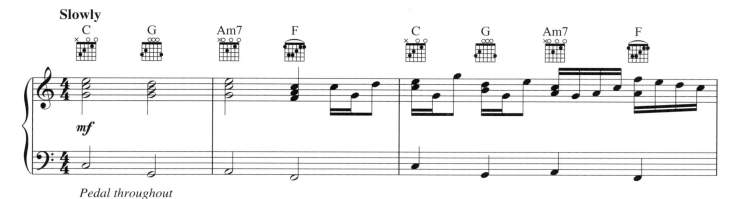

I heard from a friend to-day __ and she said you were __ in town. __ Sud-den-

ly the mem-o-ries came back to me in my mind. _____ How can

ALL FOR YOU

Words and Music by JANET JACKSON,
JAMES HARRIS III, TERRY LEWIS, WAYNE GARFIELD,
DAVID ROMANI and MAURO MALAVASI

Steady Dance beat

All my girls at the par - ty, look at that bod - y, shak-ing that thing like you nev-er did see. Got a

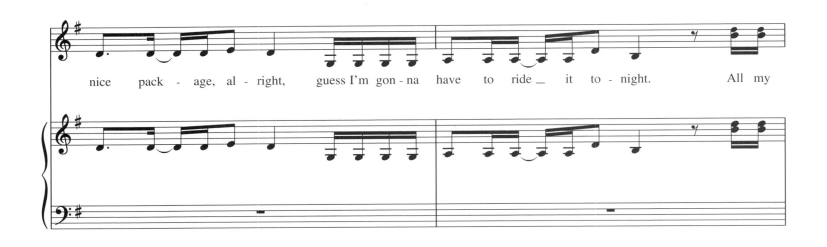

nice pack - age, al - right, guess I'm gon - na have to ride __ it to - night. All my

girls at the par - ty, look at that bod - y, shak-ing that thing like you nev - er did see. Got a

Tell me I'm the on - ly one.

Soon you'll be hav - ing fun.

Come o - ver here and get some.

Soon you'll be hav - ing fun.

BLACK CAT

Words and Music by
JANET JACKSON

Driving Rock

All the lone - ly nights   I spend a -
er, boy, but just at a glance. _

lone. _   Nev - er 'round   to love me,   you're al - ways   gone, _   'cause you're hang -
_   You'll do an - y - thing if   giv - en a   chance. _   Schem - ing, plan -

in' out   break - in' the rules. _   Oh, the man   has come   look - in' for you. _
nin' lies   to get what you need; _   so full   of prom - is - es   that you'll nev - er

ALRIGHT

Words and Music by JANET JACKSON,
JAMES HARRIS III and TERRY LEWIS

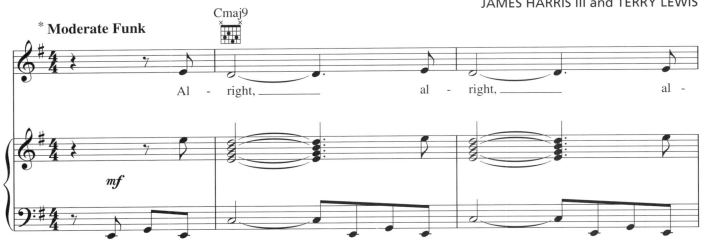

* Recorded a half step lower.

Cmaj9

See - ing ___ that your love's true, ___ nev - er I'll doubt you.
Catch a fall - in' star that shines, ___ make a wish, clap three times.

My heart ___ be - longs to you, that's al - right with me.
Dreams come true, it's in the mind, that's al - right with me.

(1., 3.) Worlds could ___ end a - round me, so in love that I can see.
(2.) Your wish ___ is my com - mand, nev - er thought I'd fall in love a - gain.

You and me were meant to be, that's al - right with me.
A - gain with my best friend, that's al - right with me.

Ah, _____ al - right _ with me. Ah, _____
(Al - right with me, al - right

_____ shoo-be-doo-be-dup, al - right _____ with me.
with me, al - right with me,

Al - right _____ with me. It's al - right, _ ba-
al - right with me.)

D.S. al Coda

- by. It's al - rı́ght, _ I tell you that it's al - right with me.

ANY TIME, ANY PLACE

Words and Music by JANET JACKSON,
JAMES HARRIS III and TERRY LEWIS

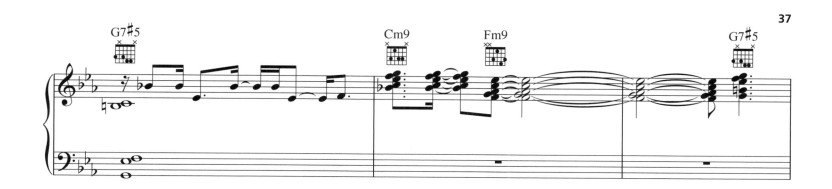

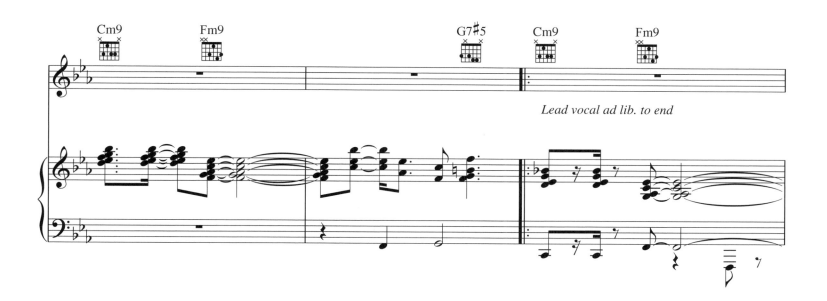

Lead vocal ad lib. to end

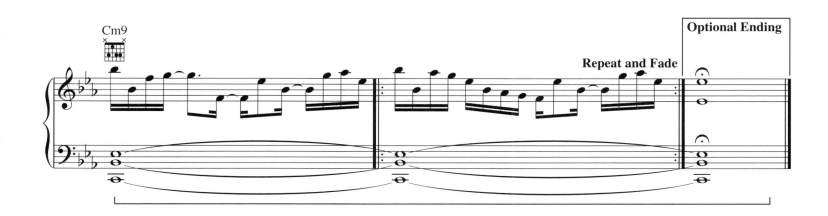

COME BACK TO ME

Words and Music by JANET JACKSON,
JAMES HARRIS III and TERRY LEWIS

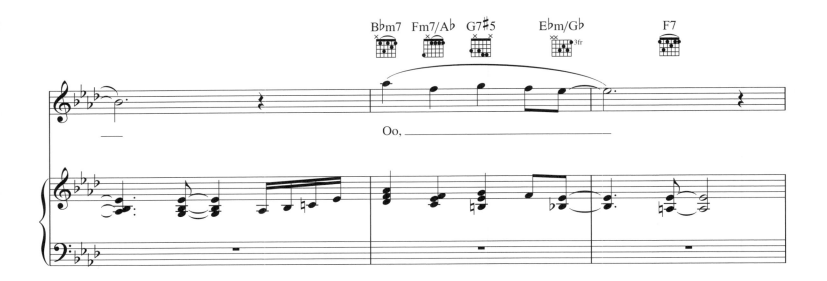

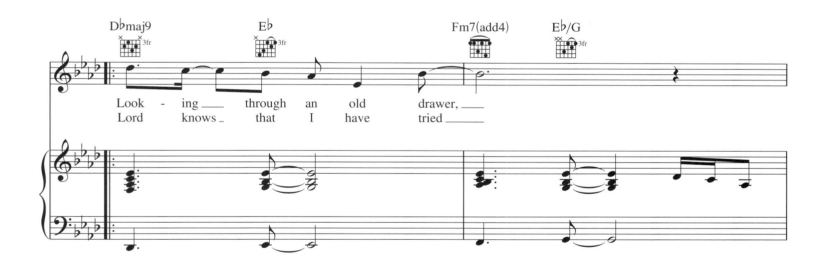

Look - ing ___ through an old drawer, ___
Lord knows ___ that I have tried _____

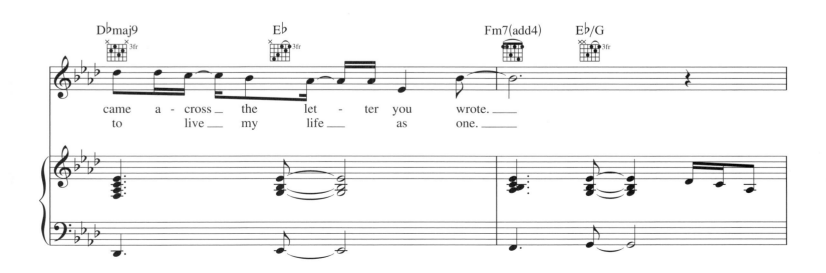

came a - cross ___ the let - ter you wrote. ___
to live ___ my life ___ as one. ___

DOESN'T REALLY MATTER

from THE NUTTY PROFESSOR II: THE KLUMPS

Words and Music by JANET JACKSON,
JAMES HARRIS III and TERRY LEWIS

ESCAPADE

Words and Music by JANET JACKSON,
JAMES HARRIS III and TERRY LEWIS

Medium Dance groove

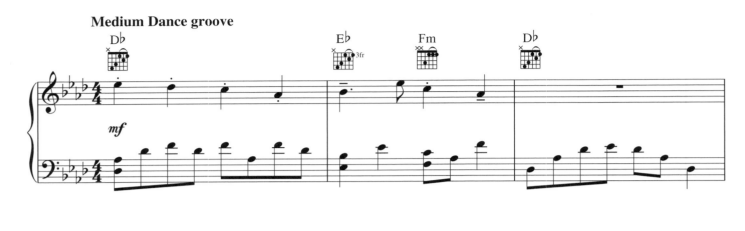

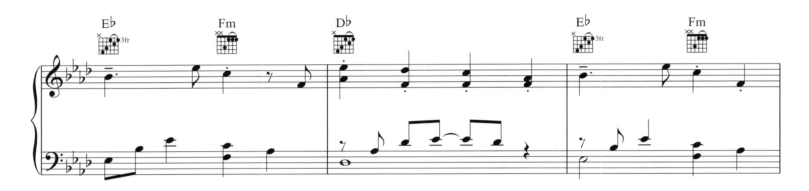

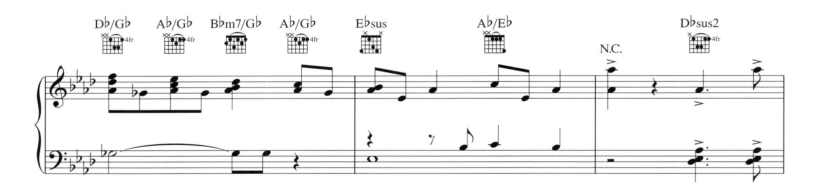

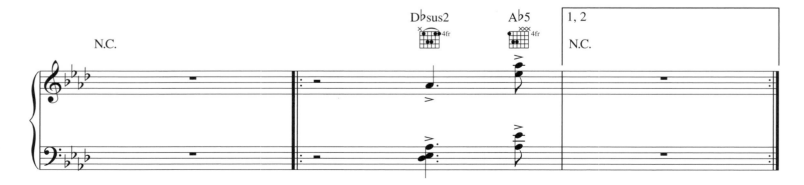

I GET LONELY

Words and Music by JANET JACKSON, JAMES HARRIS III,
TERRY LEWIS and RENE ELIZONDO JR.

IF

Words and Music by JANET JACKSON, JAMES HARRIS III,
TERRY LEWIS, HARVEY FUQUA, JOHN BRISTOL and JACKEY BEAVERS

LET'S WAIT AWHILE

Words and Music by JANET JACKSON,
JAMES HARRIS III, TERRY LEWIS and MELANIE ANDREWS

Rock Ballad

There's some-thin' I want __ to tell _____ you. There's
we get to know __ each oth _____ er, and

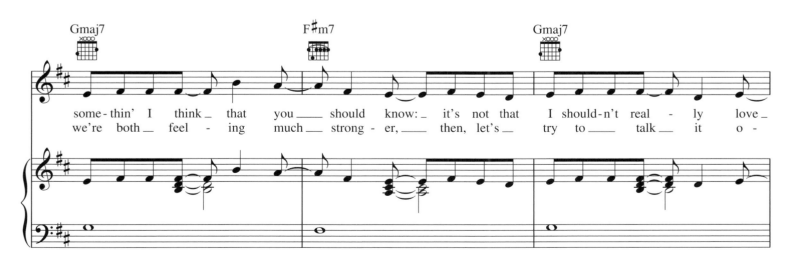

some-thin' I think __ that you ____ should know: it's not that I should-n't real - ly love
we're both ____ feel - ing much ____ strong - er, ____ then, let's ____ try to ____ talk __ it o -

LOVE WILL NEVER DO
(Without You)

Words and Music by JAMES HARRIS III
and TERRY LEWIS

NASTY

Words and Music by JAMES HARRIS III,
TERRY LEWIS and JANET JACKSON

MISS YOU MUCH

Words and Music by JAMES HARRIS III
and TERRY LEWIS

Shot _____ like an ar - row through my heart, _

Recorded a half step lower.

That's the pain I feel, ___ I feel when-ev - er

we're a - part. ___ Not to say that I'm in love ___ with you, ___
I'm rush - ing home ___

but who's to say that I'm not. ___ I just know that it
just as soon as I can. ___ I'm rush - ing home to see your

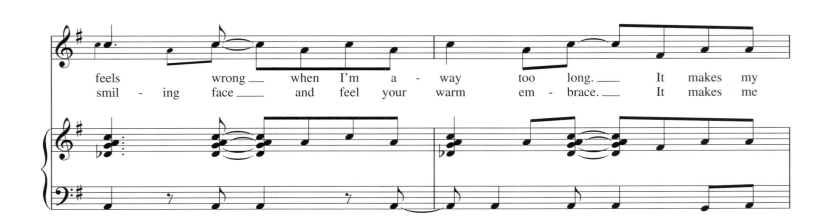

feels wrong ___ when I'm a - way too long. ___ It makes my
smil - ing face ___ and feel your warm em - brace. ___ It makes me

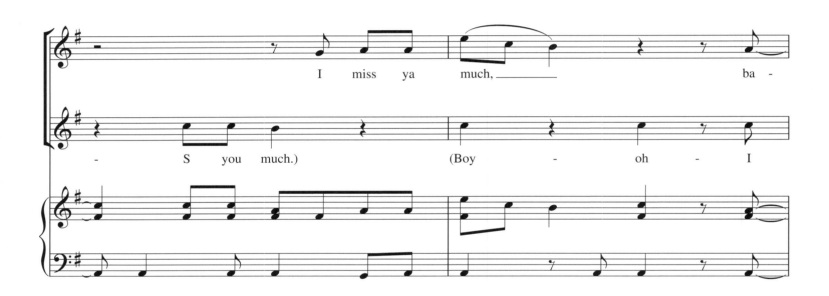

RHYTHM NATION

Words and Music by JANET JACKSON,
JAMES HARRIS III and TERRY LEWIS

-cial in-jus - tice. ___ A gen - er - a - tion full ___ of cour-

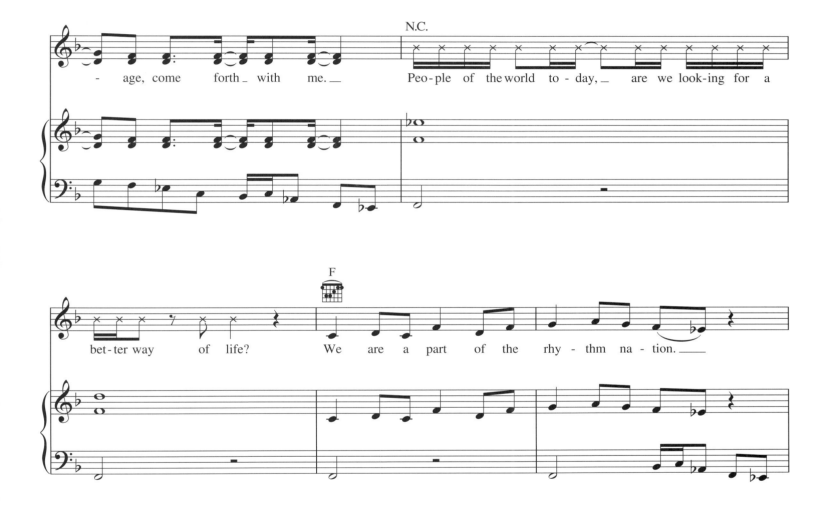

-age, come forth ___ with me. ___ Peo-ple of the world to-day, ___ are we look-ing for a

N.C.

F

bet-ter way of life? We are a part of the rhy - thm na - tion. ___

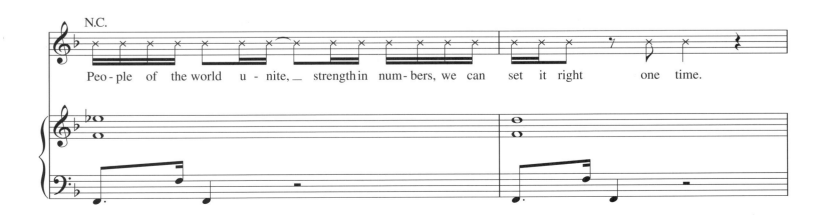

N.C.

Peo-ple of the world u - nite, ___ strength in num - bers, we can set it right one time.

It's time_ to give_ a damn. Let's work_ to-geth - er,_ come on_ now.

Peo - ple of the world to - day, _ are we look-ing for a bet - ter way of life?

We are a part of the rhy - thm na - tion. _____

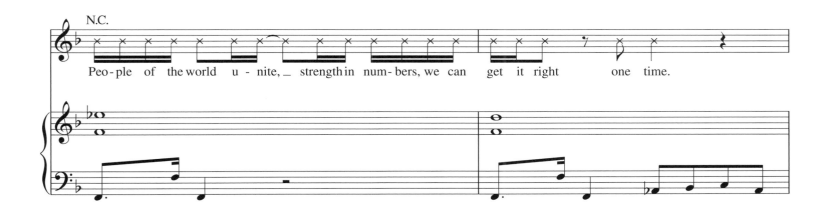

Peo - ple of the world u - nite, _ strength in num-bers, we can get it right one time.

RUNAWAY

Words and Music by JANET JACKSON,
JAMES HARRIS III and TERRY LEWIS

Moderately slow

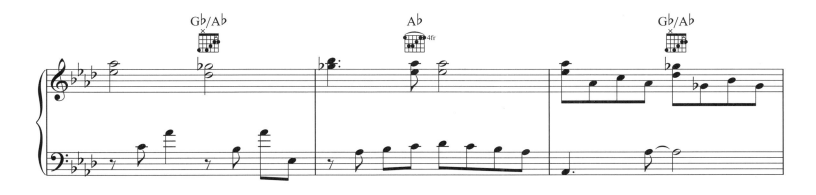

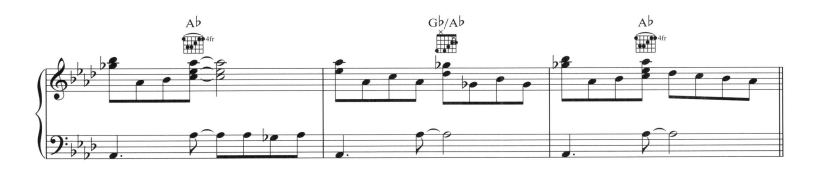

I've seen the world, been to man - y plac - es.

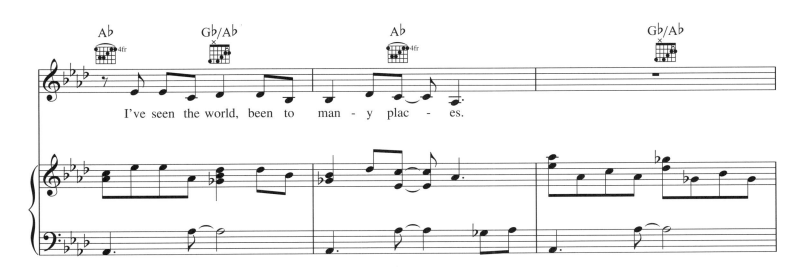

SOMEONE TO CALL MY LOVER

Words and Music by JANET JACKSON,
JAMES HARRIS III, TERRY LEWIS and DEWEY BUNNELL

Back on the road a- gain, feel- ing kind of lone- ly and look- ing for the right guy___

spoil them when I'm in love, giv- ing them what they dream of. Some- times it's not a good thing,

THAT'S THE WAY LOVE GOES

Words and Music by JANET JACKSON, JAMES HARRIS III, TERRY LEWIS,
JAMES BROWN, FRED WESLEY, CHARLES BOBBIT and JOHN STARKS

Moderate R&B

TOGETHER AGAIN

Words and Music by JANET JACKSON,
TERRY LEWIS and JAMES HARRIS III

WHEN I THINK OF YOU

Words and Music by JAMES HARRIS III,
TERRY LEWIS and JANET JACKSON

Moderately fast

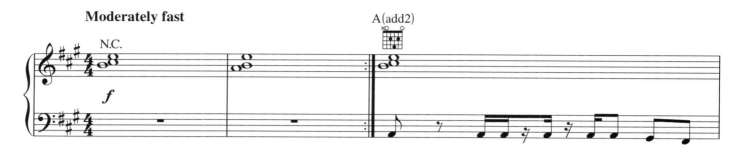

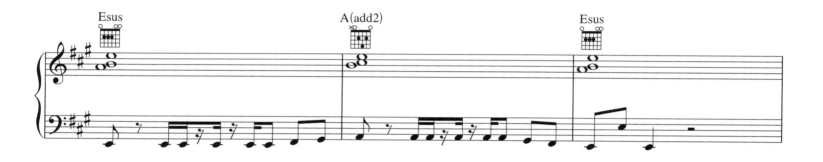

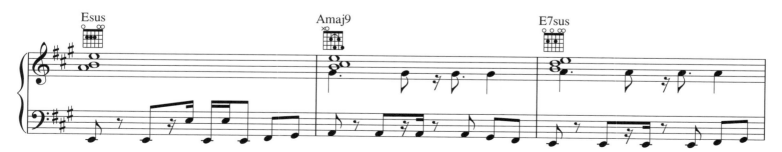

So in love. So in love. So in love.

(Lead vocal ad lib.)

Play 3 times

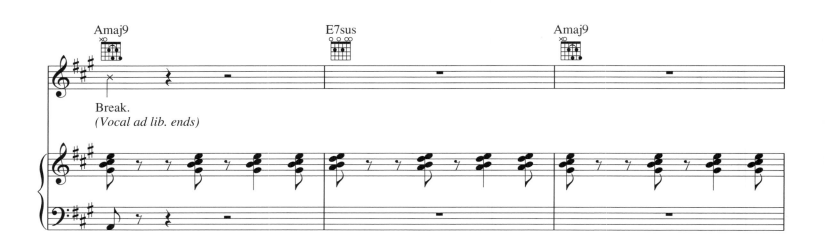

Break.
(Vocal ad lib. ends)

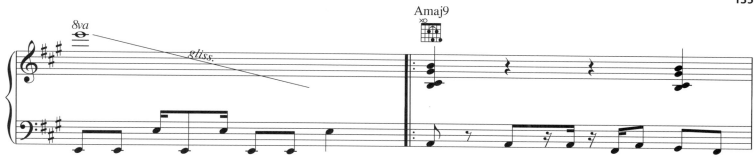

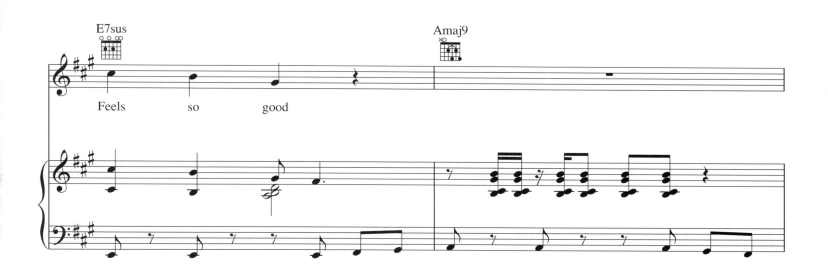

Feels so good

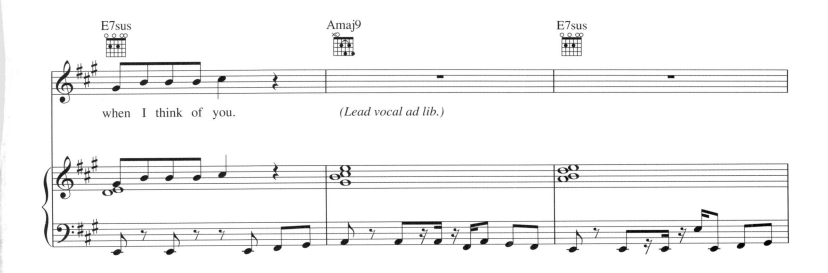

when I think of you.

(Lead vocal ad lib.)

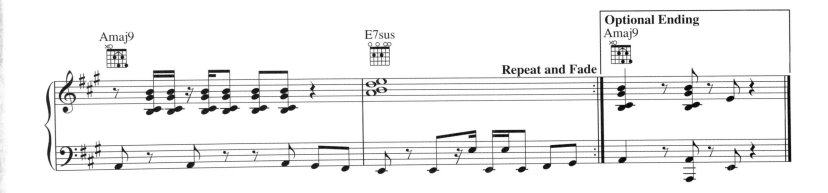

Optional Ending

Repeat and Fade